THE MEANWOOD VILLAGE ASSOCIATION PRESENTS

MEANWOOD
IN
PICTURES

A delightful painting of the Meanwood Institute after the extensive renovation works in the early 1990s.   Artist Sue Bourne.

VOLUME 2 — 1960s to 1999

Compiled by
PETER BEWELL

Assisted by
BRYN EVANS, ARTHUR HOPWOOD and DOREEN WOOD

Published by
M.V.A.Publications

95, Green Road
Meanwood
Leeds LS6 4LE

First published 2005

ISBN 0 9547946 2 1

Printed and bound by
Smith Settle Printing and Bookbinding Ltd
Ilkley Road, Otley, Leeds LS21 3JP

ACKNOWLEDGEMENTS

The majority of the photographs in this volume are from the Bewell Collection of prints and colour slides which are now held in the archives of the Meanwood Village Association.

Other prints have been provided by the following, to whom the Association records its grateful thanks; Peggy Ashton, Eileen Barratt, Bentley Court, Harold Best, Bentley Primary School, Sue Bourne, John Bilbrough, Barbara Blakeney, Anne Burgess, Carr Manor Primary School, Winifred Chapman, Alan Clift, Anne Coates, Martin Cockerill, Betty D'Ambrosio, Revd Stanley Dodd, Keith Denney, Dorothy Fenton, Roy Hall, Barbara Hill, Arthur Hopwood, Nan Kinder, Brenda Lancaster, Peter Langley, Meanwood C. of E. Primary School, Miles Hill Primary School, Frances Needham, Miss Pearson, Janet Pouncey, M.E.N.A., Sue Reddington, Graham Walker, Dennis Wrigglesworth and Yorkshire Post Newspapers.

Thanks also to all those who helped in any way in the production of this volume.

MEANWOOD

"The Village within a City"

Following the success of Volume 1, which was published in 2004, we have pleasure in presenting Volume 2 which covers the four decades from the 1960s up to 1999.

We have tried to record the many changes which have taken place in this period, both in the physical changes to the area and in the lifestyles of its residents.

In the early years of this period the demolition craze still raged on, but then there was a change of mood and people became more conservation minded resulting in the saving of Tannery Square, some cottages on Parkside Road, Hollin Lane Farm and later the Tannery.

By 1999, the old corner shops had virtually disappeared, being replaced with the supermarkets of Netto, G.T.Smith, (later to become the Co-op) and Aldi.

Shopping patterns changed, as the advent of fridges and freezers meant that people no longer had to shop frequently for fresh produce.

During the years covered by this book a number of fast-food outlets, ethnic food shops and cafes have sprung up in Meanwood. Milkmen however have almost disappeared from our streets.

Home conditions have changed beyond all recognition. Central heating, double glazing, microwave ovens, televisions, washing machines, dishwashers, mobile phones and computers now being the norm.

Following the introduction of the Clean Air Act in 1956, the benefits became apparent in the 60s and 70s, so that we no longer suffer the awful fogs and attendant grime which emanated from thousands of coal fires. For example, if you stand on Sugarwell Hill you can now see right across the valley and the city, which you certainly could not have done in the past.

Industry almost disappeared in the period, with the closure of the Tannery and Yorkshire Switchgear and Meanwood now is largely a residential suburb of Leeds with the Bentleys, Monk Bridges and Highburys having many student residents.

Landmark chimneys at Bateson's Tannery, the Meanwood Road Destructor and the main Tannery all fell to the demolition men. The Destructor site is now a modern reclamation centre.

Housing too has seen vast changes. The large estates of ' White Houses' in the Stonegates, Stainbecks and Farm Hills were demolished and replaced with a mixture of local authority and private developments. New local authority estates were built on Seven Sisters Hill (The Beckhills), plus some small developments along Green Road. The King Alfred's estate was modernised. Private and Housing Association developments such as the Boothroyds (Switchgear site), The Wickets, (behind the Working Men's Club), Greenwood Park, (Beckett Home), Badger Wood (off Parkside Road), Church Lane Mews

(Brick Row), have been constructed. A large estate,(the Woodleas) now occupies the former hospital site and what was farmland off Church Lane became the Holmwoods.

A modern Vicarage was built on the site of the large Victorian one.

Sheltered Housing has been provided at Bentley Court and Memorial Drive.

Health care has changed, with the building of a large comprehensive Health Centre at the top end of Meanwood Road and a new day care centre at Millside off Monk Bridge Road. Meanwood Park Hospital however was closed down and the residents dispersed into the community.

New schools have appeared at Tongue Lane, Beckhill, and Carr Manor.

The Church of England Primary School in Green Road was modernised and extended in the early 1990s, but sadly, Bentley Lane Primary School was closed in 2004, (although the buildings are still used as temporary accommodation for other schools).

The Meanwood Institute was completely refurbished in 1993/4 and facilities extended by local volunteers. It is now a well-used venue for various community activities and private parties.

A new venture, the Meanwood Valley Urban Farm, was created where the old rhubarb fields were on Sugarwell Hill. It is now a very popular place for school visits and families with children.

A big new David Lloyd Sports Centre was built near the Ring Road off Tongue Lane.

The Community Centre on Stainbeck Avenue was redeveloped and now offers various community facilities. Meanwood Elders Neighbourhood Action (M.E.N.A.), the organisation catering for the elderly and Meanwood Valley Baptists are based there.

The number of vehicles has increased enormously. With most families now having at least one car, traffic congestion is commonplace. New traffic lights and roundabouts have been necessary. Street lighting has changed for the better and the gas lamps of the 1960s are long gone.

Having listed some of the big changes, it is pleasing to record also that there are still many things which have not changed. The Churches are still there, albeit with reduced congregations. Hustler's Row, Tannery Square, and various old cottages remain and are much sought after. The Conservative Club and The Working Men's Club are still going strong. The Meanwood pub was demolished and the Beckett's Arms has closed, but The Myrtle and the Bay Horse continue as pubs offering food. Meanwood Cricket Club still play on their ground near the Myrtle pub on Parkside Road. Woodhouse also continue to play at their ground in Meanwood Road but, sadly, Highbury Cricket Club wound up at the end of 2004. Meanwoodside, and walks through the valley to the Seven Arches and Adel are as popular as ever and the dam at the Tannery is still a popular fishing spot.

In short, Meanwood is still alive and well, with a strong community spirit.

I hope you enjoy looking at the pictures and reading the comments in this volume as much as you did the first one.

Peter Bewell.
2005.

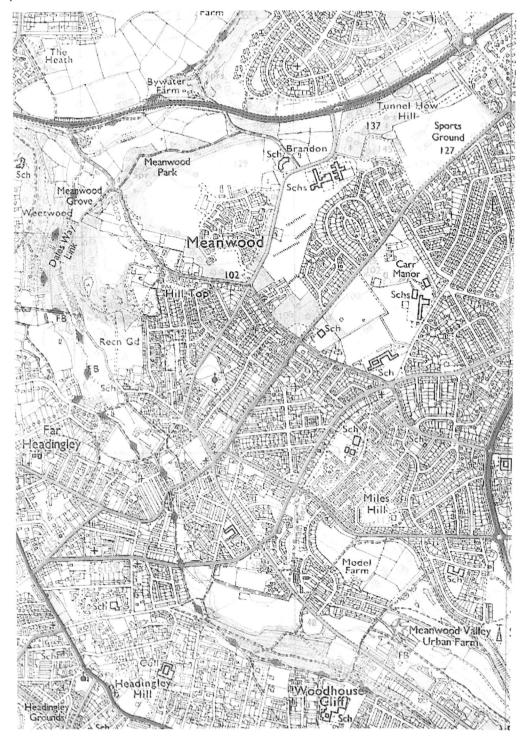

Map of Meanwood compiled in the 1990s with the hospital site partly developed. The green diamonds trace the route of the Dales Way Link winding its way through the valley from Woodhouse towards the Seven Arches. By following this route you would eventually finish up at Bowness in the Lake District. (Printed under licence from Ordnance Survey.)

An aerial photograph from 1980.

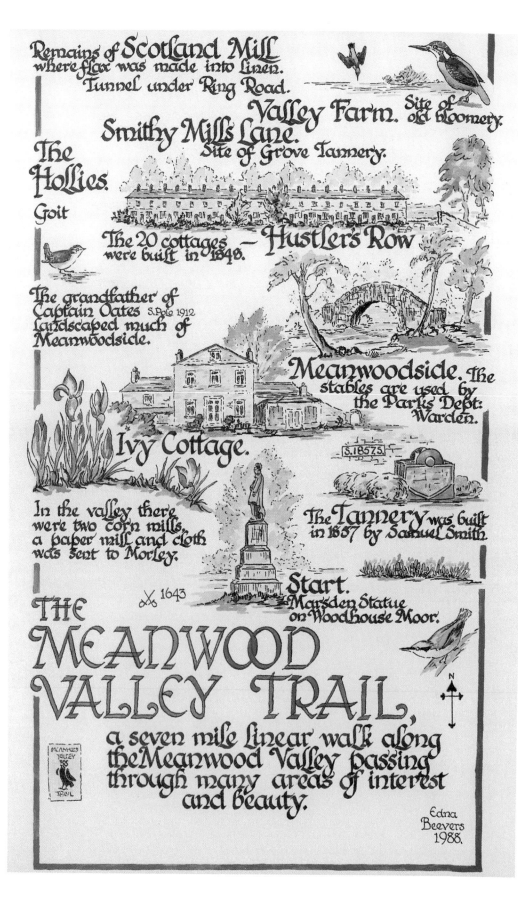

Remains of Scotland Mill where flax was made into linen.
Tunnel under Ring Road.

Valley Farm. Site of old bloomery.

Smithy Mills Lane.
Site of Grove Tannery.

The Hollies.

Goit

The 20 cottages were built in 1848. — Hustler's Row

The grandfather of Captain Oates S.Pole 1912 landscaped much of Meanwoodside.

Meanwoodside. The stables are used by the Parks Dept: Warden.

Ivy Cottage.

S. 1857 S.

In the valley there were two corn mills, a paper mill and cloth was sent to Morley.

The Tannery was built in 1857 by Samuel Smith.

1643

Start.
Marsden Statue on Woodhouse Moor.

THE MEANWOOD VALLEY TRAIL,
a seven mile linear walk along the Meanwood Valley passing through many areas of interest and beauty.

N

Edna Beevers 1988.

The trail ends at Golden Acre Park.
Ornamental trees & shrubs,
a lake and
The Bakery Coffee House
repaired and renovated
by boys of the d.O.P. 1982.

Adel Dam
nature
reserve.

Five Lane Ends.
The Leeds Country
Way crosses here.

Goff Farm Cottage.
Stairfoot Lane.

← To
Adel
Church.

To →
Eccup
Res.

At the
Slabbering Baby
Spring there was
an open air cafe.

Adel Crag.

Old dam wall.

Seven Arches Aqueduct 1840.
Iron main 1866.

A beautiful linear painting from 1988 by Edna Beevers, illustrating the route of the Meanwood Valley Trail. A very popular walk through the beautiful valley with its multitude of flora and fauna.

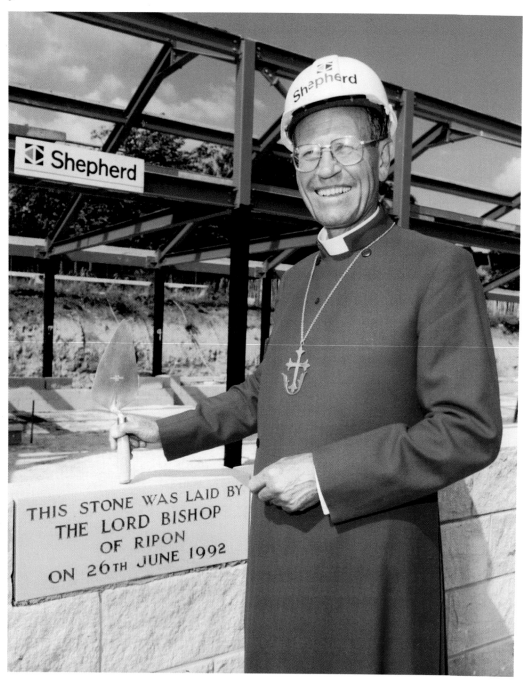

A happy picture of DAVID, BISHOP OF RIPON, when he laid the foundation stone of the new school extension in Green Road. The Victorian section of the school was modernised and new buildings constructed at the rear. The Governors had to raise 15% of the total cost of £1m, so the 'Meanwood School Building Appeal' (M.S.B.A.) was launched in 1989. By means of a whole range of fundraising activities M.S.B.A. raised the £150,000 needed in only 1,273 days, a cause which was widely supported by the community. A very busy, but happy period in the life of Meanwood.

A photograph of Her Majesty The Queen as she was driven along the Ring Road near the bottom of Dunny Hill on her way to Harewood House in the 1960s.

Her Royal Highness Princess Alexandra, at the official opening of the Bentley Court sheltered housing project in Bentley Lane on 21st September 1994.

'Daisy Bank', the large house at the junction of Church Lane and Green Road just before demolition.

The last of the 'White Houses' on the Stonegate Estate being demolished in January 1993.

CRASH! Down comes the house on the steep part of Church Lane where the Hopwood family once lived. 1964.

1986, and here in Meanwood Road we see the demolition of part of the Wharfedales to create a landscaped area.

A sad period in 1980 when the much-loved Capitol cinema, the ballroom and adjacent shops 'bit the dust'. In earlier years the cinema (shown on the front cover) was the main entertainment centre in the community and queues for admission were the norm. Saturday afternoon matinees were extremely popular with the children and known as 'the tuppenny rush'. In later years the Capitol became a Bingo Hall. The ballroom too was very popular, with young people coming from all over Leeds to dance to the music of Bert Noble and Jack Mann. On a Saturday night, queues would form the length of the shopping parade by 6 p.m. to buy tickets for the 8 p.m. dance. Many a romance (including the author's) began there!
Midweek dances were also held and the Chapel, for example, held a monthly one on Wednesday evenings in the winter. In 1962 the Chapel held its stewardship campaign dinner there. It was also a very popular venue for wedding receptions, particularly from the chapel which was only a 50 yard walk away.
Its popularity declined, and in 1968 the ballroom closed and reopened as a night club known as 'The Cat's Whiskers'. Finally a big new G.T.Smith (later the Co-op) supermarket, some shops and a Yorkshire Bank were built on the site.

A winter scene at the bottom of the Hollies in 1994.

Sledging in the park in 1969.

A lovely display of crocuses in the garden of Ivy Cottage on Green Road.

Spring colour in the Hollies in 1990.

The bridge over the beck in Meanwoodside in autumn 1974. The road which it originally carried ran from Green Road, behind Ivy Cottage, through to Hollin Lane.

Another autumn scene in 1974 further up the beck, with Hustler's Row in the background.

The beck has been, and still is, a very popular place with children and here we see some of them with their dog 'larking about' on the weir in 1987.

The one that didn't make it. Trouble when he arrived home no doubt !

Holy Trinity Church in the evening light in 1993.

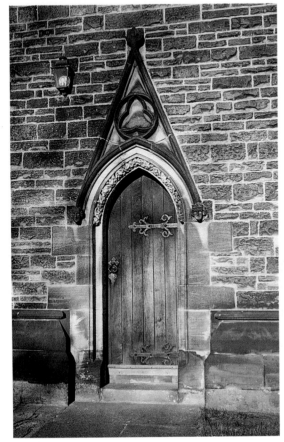

The vestry door to the Church.

The Lych Gate leading into Church Lane from the churchyard.

The mausoleum of the Beckett family in the churchyard. It featured in the television series of 'A Touch of Frost'.

Flower Festivals have long been a tradition at the church and these three photographs show displays from the 1992 Festival.

The Revd Stanley Dodd became Vicar of Meanwood in 1965 and continued in post until the 30th July 1989.

Our pictures, taken on that final day, show:

top left: *Children from the youth organisations in the church doorway.*

top right: *Stanley and his wife Anne arriving at the church.*

left: *The Vicar in his robes.*

Sandra Glassby - Enrolling Member and Marion Mann - Presiding Member for Headingley Deanery, with an exhibition of work from the Mothers' Union in 1995.

Double celebration. Frances Grose on her 90th birthday with the Revd Richard Wiggen on his 50th on 24th May 1992.

The Revd Stanley Dodd with former pupils of the Leeds College of Commerce who held their 50 years reunion in 1989. Nina Stainthorpe, Lady Steele (formerly Barbara Harrison) and Dorothy Fenton (nee Thackray).

A flower arrangement at the 1999 Festival in church commemorating Dorothy Fenton's wartime confirmation in 1940.

Doris Thackray celebrating her 90th birthday in December 1987.

The Hoyland twins in their Robin Hood outfits after the ecumenical trip to Epworth and Clumber Park in 1991.

Who's the lucky raffle winner then? By the look on the Vicar's face it must have been him!

Members of the Royal British Legion parade along Parkside Road in November 1982.

The 1st Meanwood Guide Company in the same parade.

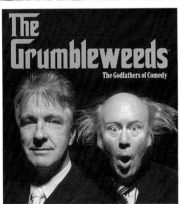

'THE GRUMBLEWEEDS' the well known comedy music group was formed in November 1962 and had its origins in Meanwood. Graham Walker lived in Church Lane, Maurice Lee in Stonegate Farm Road, Albert and Carl Sutcliffe both worked at the Yorkshire Switchgear and Robin Colville lived in nearby Headingley. In their early years they practised in the Parochial Hall and performed at the Beckett's Arms and the Working Men's Club.

below: Graham is seen here when he came to judge the Teddy Bear's Picnic at Ivy Cottage, one of the events celebrating the 150th Anniversary of Meanwood C. of E. Primary School in 1990.

Commonly known as 'THE BLOBS', the Bentley Lane Old Boys Association was formed a few years ago and meet every few months for a pleasant reunion over a pub meal. Pictured here are Tommy Clifford, Don Hargreaves, Terry Richardson, John Bilbrough (organiser), Selwyn Levin, Brian Horsey, John Sykes, John Collinson and Malcolm Dent.

Another local music group was 'THE MIXED FEELINGS' seen here practising in the old Meanwood quarry in 1968 before it was filled in. Richard Hughes, Stephen Ashton, Andrew Dunderdale and Willy Ling (now a well known photographer).

The Beck has always featured in the Meanwood story. In times long past it provided essential power for numerous mills and tanneries along its course. Over the years there have been a number of disputes regarding the jealously guarded water rights along the beck.

In more recent times it has provided a pleasant feature in the valley much loved by walkers. Two of our pictures in 1974 show it in a tranquil mood with autumn leaves floating along. The third and fourth photographs taken in 1976 shows what the beck can be like following heavy rain; a number of tragedies have occurred here over the years.

The view over the city from Sugarwell Hill in 1968. You can see the destructor chimney and some of the newly built multi-storey flats.

A 1974 view of the gateway to Meanwood Park on Green Road.

Looking up Church Lane from its junction with Green Road. The white building a little way up on the left is the original Methodist Chapel, later to become a laundry, a builders' merchants and finally a glass company. (Now being converted into dwellings).

The Church Drive seen from Green Road in 1976, prior to it being developed as a sheltered housing scheme.

One of the clapper bridges (big stone slabs) over the beck in Meanwoodside.

A little known old packhorse bridge at the bottom of Woodhouse Ridge behind what is now the Boothroyd estate. Thought to be on a trade route from Leeds to an old industrial site in the Meanwood Valley.

Ivy Cottage on Green Road has been the venue for many events and fund raising garden parties over the years for the Chapel, Church and School. The photographs here, show some of the stalls in the garden in 1972, and the record crowd of 440 at the 'Teddy Bear's Picnic' in 1990.

Mr. Bumby talking to members of the Meanwood Village Association on Hustler's Row in 1982.

The Revd Alan Powers, Minister at the Methodist Church from 1974 until 1982 on the 1976 M.V.A.Easter walk.

Members of the M.V.A. wend their way through Meanwoodside on an Easter Tuesday afternoon walk in 1976. These walks became a tradition of the Association and continue to this day.

The same party a little further on, with Hustler's Row in the background.

left and below:
Members on the 1979 walk, which took us to the top of Woodhouse Ridge.

In 1980 we 'Beat the Bounds' around the Parish of Meanwood and are seen here to the north of King Alfred's Castle. The brown field just behind the walkers is now the site of the David Lloyd Sports Centre and has been well landscaped. Beyond that, adjacent to the Ring Road, is now the big shopping centre including Sainsbury's and Homebase .

The walk in 1982 was up the valley to Adel church where Alf Stead is seen explaining details of the church.

Fred Casperson, who with Arthur Hopwood wrote the history book about Meanwood, (see inside back cover) talking to members on the site of the big house in Meanwoodside. (Sadly demolished in the 1950s.)

In 1995 we had quite a change and instead of a country walk we had a guided tour around the city centre.

Carr Manor was the venue for 1996 where we had a fascinating tour of the grounds and the house.

Some photographs of M.V.A. members, taken on the walks.

top: *Linda Thwaites and Les and Marion Mann.*

bottom: *Frank Ashton and Harold Bradbury.*

The Association has held various exhibitions over the years, and here are three photographs taken at the 1999 photographic exhibition in the Parochial Hall. The exhibitions never fail to bring in the crowds, who are always fascinated by the old photographs and documents.

A view of members crossing the bridge in Meanwoodside in 1976, with Hustler's Row in the background.

Children from Stainbeck United Reformed Church at their garden party in July 1989.

Stainbeck ladies, serving in the café in 1986, having a welcome break.

Stainbeck children in the cast of 'Just One Cornetto', a pantomime written and produced by Church members in 1978.

In 1977 they are seen here in 'The Magic Feather'.

44

A very realistic setting for a nativity play. The barn on the Meanwood Valley Urban Farm.

Happy children and staff with a goat at the farm.

Christopher Timothy, the actor, is a Patron of the farm and has always shown a keen interest in its activities. Here he is seen being filmed in the stables.

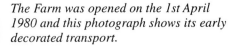

Sue Reddington the Farm Director with Bill Kilgallon the Lord Mayor of Leeds with two of the latest arrivals at the farm.

The Farm was opened on the 1st April 1980 and this photograph shows its early decorated transport.

This 'state of the art' environmentally friendly timber building known as 'THE EPICENTRE' was officially opened on 15ᵗʰ September 1999 by the Rt.Hon. Michael Meacher M.P. The farm is visited by many school parties and families and is well worth a visit.

Members of the Meanwood Men's Society, which meets fortnightly in the winter months, are seen here on a family Christmas walk at Bolton Abbey in 1999. Peter and Pat Spedding with children Grace and Anna, Jackie Brewer, Barbara Blakeney, Margaret Jackson, Roy Tulloch, Christine and Peter Bewell, Val Milner and Sheila Stephenson.

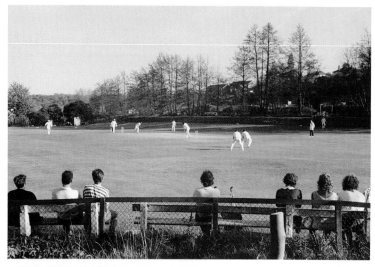

Cricket being played on Highbury Works pitch, May 1989. Sadly, after many years, the club ceased to exist at the end of the 2004 season.

The Bowling Club in Meanwood Park is still going strong and members are seen here in May 1992.

Meanwood Elderly Neighbourhood Action (M.E.N.A.) is based at the Community Centre in Stainbeck Avenue and do much good work in organising events for the elderly. Members are seen here with a large tapestry which they had made.

Some of the ladies enjoying a meal on one of their outings.

Another group pictured on one of their regular theatre visits.

The Women's Institute celebrated its 70th anniversary on the 21st March 1989 and three of their Presidents are seen here at its Jubilee dinner. Edith Robinson, Joan Stead and Irene King.

A group of W.I. ladies planting a tree at Skelton Grange in 1994.

The Committee in 1997 with a New Zealand visitor, Collen Young.

Lord Grimthorpe, a descendant of the founder of the Church of England School in Green Road, on the occasion of the official opening of the courtyard on 22nd April 1994.

A milestone day for the school when the new building was officially handed over. Revd Richard Wiggen- Chairman of the Governors, Bryn Evans- Headteacher, and Brett Gaunt- Architect .

Alf Stead reading at the lectern in church in 1967 where he had been the Parish Clerk and Verger for 37 years.

At a special service on 7th October 1997 at Holy Trinity Meanwood, David, Bishop of Ripon admitted and licensed Frances Needham to the office of Reader. We see her here being congratulated by the Vicar, the Revd Richard Wiggen.

'A man of letters!'
Dennis Wrigglesworth, the postman who had plodded the Meanwood patch for 27 years seemed to know everyone and everything that was going on in the area. Often referred to as 'Dennis the Post' he was the winner of the regional prize for 'Postie of the Year' in 1993 and went on into the national finals. He is pictured here with Rene Stephens who nominated him.

Dennis, in 1978, when Jean Turner made a presentation to him on behalf of the residents of Greenwood Mount on the occasion of his marriage. Included in the picture are Nellie Salmon, two Miss Oswalds, Billie Hearn, Betty D'Ambrosio, Clara Batty, Sheila Wright, Mrs. Cook and Mrs. Bracewell.

George Albert Chapman, known as Skipper, or Skip, amongst the scouting fraternity. In 1935 he became the leader of the Rover Scouts at the Methodist Church. Then in 1937, with the assistance of Harold Holland, formed a scout group at Meanwood Park Hospital which catered for the mentally handicapped. As well as his scouting activities, he played

in the Methodist Church cricket and football teams and was a keen motorcyclist. (A ride on his pillion was a real treat!). His devotion to the scouts at the hospital was rightly recognised in October 1967 by the award of the British Empire Medal and he is seen here with his mother proudly showing his decoration.

Fellow scouters congratulating Skipper were Ron Jefferies, Graham Slade, Brian Cahill, Derek Olliver, Clifford Turner, Arthur Hopwood, Betty Clark, Nellie Salmon, and Harold Holland.

The 31st. N.W.Leeds Scout Group at Meanwood Park Hospital (previously known as The Colony). Leaders on the left were George Chapman and Ron Jefferies, and on the right Harold Holland and Len ('Ligger') Lister. They were twinned with the 8th N.W. Meanwood Methodist scout group and were seen every month parading round Meanwood with their combined bands leading the Youth Organisations.

Arthur Hopwood photographing the re-roofing work on the Meanwood Institute in August 1987.

*Members of the Institute in the snooker room, just before the major refurbishment began in 1993.
Lionel Perfect, Max Perfect, John Barnes, Ben Wormald, George Cockrill, Harold Bradbury, Bob
Marshall, Ken Benton, Frank Thompson,   ?, John Stewart, Cyril Brown, Frank Sheard, George
Wiseman.*

In 1993 the Institute was in a very poor state of repair and the snooker tables were sinking through the floor! A fund-raising campaign was started to raise money for materials and a team of volunteers carried out extensive works. The scene here is in the snooker room where amongst various works new concrete foundations for the tables were laid.

Jim Durrant, Frank Ashton and Max Perfect laying the new floor in the front room which was named 'The Meanwood Room'.

Jim Durrant sorts the plumbing.

Alan Corners building the new toilet block.

A piece of history preserved. This is the winding gear which was used to lower and raise a wooden partition which divided the front room. Now in a display case in the entrance.

Happy worker, Jack Mathers.

The Institute was the venue for an unusual (unique?) event when, as part of the Meanwood School Building Appeal, ten men from the Meanwood Trinity Men's Society staged a SNOOKERTHON. They solicited lots of sponsorship from far and wide, and raised £807. They had to play snooker continuously for 24 hours with the ladies and friends providing plenty of encouragement, food and drinks throughout the period. The lads at the Crucible had nothing to fear however as the highest break was 25 (by Alan Corners !). John Freer, Peter Bewell, Tony Taylor, Peter Smithson, Pete Spedding, Roy Tulloch, Graham David, Harold Bradbury and Alan Corners.

Play in progress.

Class group of 1972 at Meanwood Church of England School with Miss Fenton and Mr. Ashworth (Headteacher).

Another class of 1972 with Mr. Ashworth and Mrs. Ann Dunderdale (nee Vaughan).

Class group of 1975 with Mr. Ashworth and Mrs. Waud.

Moving on to 1984/5 we see the children with Mr. Evans the Headteacher and Mrs Burgess the Deputy Headteacher.
Back row; Adam Warren, Michael Eltringham, Robert Watson, James Pearson, Nichola Queenan, Lynn Hartshorne, Joanne Else.
2nd row; David Thornton, Helen McHugh, Philip Speight, Joanne Sollitt, Michael Enever, Lisa Atha, Christopher Hall, Alex Giuntoni.
3rd row; Rachel Crimp, Craig Cuthbert, Stewart Dobson, Claire Cook, Ian Harman, Clare Smith, Jamie Charlesworth.
Front row; Graham Priestley, Glenn Haigh, Claire Kettlewell, Fiona Scott, Gail Jackson, Hannah Wilson, ..?.., Daniel Elliot.

Miles Hill Primary School which was opened in 1969.

Children bringing their harvest gifts in 1969.

Children anxious to be in the picture. The new school can be seen in the background.

When the school opened there was still some work outstanding. Here we see the children supervising the workmen!

Inquisitive!

Harold Holland and Malcolm
Scholey,

Nancy Clark and Nellie
Hopwood. (Cub mistresses).

Fred Campey and Sidney
Holstead.

Fred Gamble
(Commissioner), Winifred
Chapman and Duncan
Jefferies.

Christopher Hopwood, Roy
Berwick, David Ibbetson and
Nigel Hopwood.

Geoff Holstead and   ?

Faces at the 50th anniversary re-union of the 8th N.W.Scout Group at the Methodist Church on
23rd. October 1982.

Richard Hall (Leader), with some of the scouts at the tuck shop on the campsite in Eskdale in 1986.

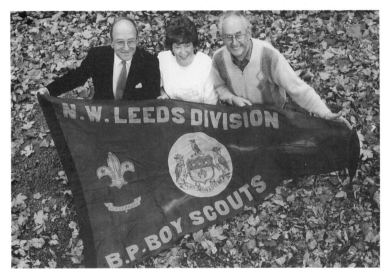

middle left: *In 1993 a scout flag dating from 1909 was unearthed in someone's attic, and here we see Peter Bewell (District Chairman), Gillian Marshall (Leader) and Arthur Hopwood (former District Commissioner) displaying it outside the Methodist Church.*

below left: *Scouts on the summit of Harter Fell on June 2nd 1988.*

below right: *Another group on top of Whernside in May 1991.*

Members of the 8th N.W. Scout Group setting off to Turnhout in Belgium on 4th August 1982 for the celebrations marking the 50th anniversary of the formation of the group and also that of the St. Victor's Group who were their hosts. The twinning of the two groups began in 1948 when the Belgian troop came to Leeds, to be followed the next year by the Meanwood troop going over there.

On July 4th 1980 six venture scouts from the 8th N.W. Group raised over £400 for the Methodist Church organ restoration fund with a sponsored expedition. Starting from sea level at Fort William they climbed the '3 Peaks', Ben Nevis, Scafell Pike and Snowdon, before touching sea level again at Caernavon 21 hours 13 minutes later, well within the 24 hour statutory time limit. Pictured here planning the route are Richard Hall, Richard Bewell, Keith Mathers, Peter Bewell (driver), David Bewell, Ian Mathers, Andrew Barratt, and Paul Hunter (driver).

The scene outside the Meanwood Institute in August 1994 during the renovation works.

Whilst excavating at the east end of the building in 1994 the workers unearthed this colourful mosaic panel. It had been in the entrance porch of the cottage adjoining the Institute and was covered in demolition material. The workers cleaned it and preserved it under the new pathway.

Bentley Lane School in October 1997.

Staff at Bentley Lane in 1996.
Front row; Alana Duncalf, Janice Ellis, Sue Backhouse, Margaret Cawsey (Headteacher),
Graham Casey (Deputy Headteacher), Susan Walker, Gill Dodsworth.
2nd. Row; Cath Heeley, Jane Milnes, Janet Seabourne, Cyndy Sharpe, Jeanette Hodgson, Jill Philp.
Back row; Annette Herron, Sheila Doherty, Susanne Tobias.

Children at Carr Manor Primary School at the Christmas concert, 8th December 1992.

Backrow:-

Mrs Druett Mr Shutt
Mrs Crossley Mr Hilton
Mrs Hargreaves Mrs Lapsley

M.Row:-

Mrs Bramber Mrs Hudson
Mrs Marsh Miss Dulin
Mrs Peters Mrs Stewart
Mrs Boyd Mrs Ingham
Mrs Dalby

Fr.Row:-

Mrs Quinn Mrs Edwards
Mrs Littlewood Mrs Payling
Mr Loye Mrs Fryer
Mrs Pickering

Staff at the school when it re-opened in October 1992.

Meanwood Church of England Primary School in 1989 prior to the refurbishment and extension.

Some of the buildings after partial demolition on 26th May 1992. The square concrete slab in the middle foreground was a new cover placed over an old well which had been found.

Rebuilding in progress, June 1992.

Workmen repointing the old stonework, 26th May 1992.

Rebuilding in progress in 1992. The old schoolhouse seen in the centre became the staffroom and offices.

Another view from the roof of the new hall showing the new buildings being constructed at the back of the original school.

Re-roofing in progress on the hall.

The time capsule which was buried under the new construction, with instructions not to be opened for 100 years ! It contained many items from 1993 such as the school prospectus, newspapers, photographs of the work, shopping leaflets, postage stamps, coins, a few acorns and various other bits and pieces which will no doubt create a lot of interest when eventually opened. What will Meanwood be like then ?

People at the Meanwood Church of England school 'Victorian Day' festivities which were part of the special 150th anniversary celebrations in May 1990.

The Lord Mayor of Leeds, Councillor Les. Carter and his wife arriving at the school in a horse drawn carriage with the Chairman of the Meanwood School Building Appeal (M.S.B.A.) Committee Peter Bewell.

Bessie Williamson and Hilda Richmond all dressed up and ready to wave their flags.

Kathy Bevons and Glynis Shaw in their finery.

Margaret Leiper, Marjorie Hopwood and Owen Hogg all dressed up for the occasion.

Henry Shaw, a former pupil, who celebrated his 100th birthday on 10th May 1991 came to visit the school on that special day and is seen here talking to children in the playground.

It must be good air in Meanwood, for here we have another centenarian, Mrs. Evelyn Danby who visited her old school in September 1997.

Children Maypole dancing in the playground at the Summer Fair .

above: *Three Headteachers, Bryn Evans,(1983 to 1998) Nan Kinder,(1977 to 1983) and Maurice Ashworth. (19..? to 1974).*

right: *Owen Hogg the school caretaker, who often went beyond the call of duty and was a great supporter of all the fundraising activities. Seen here with Janet Thornton at a Burns Night supper in the Parochial Hall.*

The Committee of M.S.B.A. nearing the end of their task in January 1993.
Seated; Anne Burgess, Margaret Leiper, Carolina Brooks, Doreen Wood, Christine Holmes,
Bev Simpson, Janice Moutsakis.
Standing; Bryn Evans, Richard Wiggen, Janet Thornton, Martin Cockerill, Barbara Blakeney,
Geoff Holland, Steve Clemmens, Peter Bewell, Peter Smithson, Jackie Brewer, Cathy Stevens,
Ian Jackson, Alan Menzies, Frank Dunderdale, Arthur Hopwood, and Alan Pedley.

ACORNS ! It started as a bit of a joke when an advert in a newspaper offered £3 per bucketful of
good fresh acorns delivered to a Tadcaster farm. However with some organisation, and the help
of many people, it turned into a money spinner for M.S.B.A. and over 3 seasons made a profit of
£1,247. Christine Bewell is seen here with the collecting barrels outside Ivy Cottage. The farm
used them to replant some oak forests which had been cut down in the First World War.

Another of the big fundraisers was a sponsored run, which brought in £2,315. Pictured here outside the supermarket are Bev Simpson, Peter Bewell ('The Scarlet Runner'), and Doreen Wood.

A picture that made it all worthwhile. Children, with teacher Heather Booth, on the first day back in the new school. 21st April 1993.

Some years earlier Jimmy
Saville came to the school
to open the Summer Fair.
He is seen here with Nan
Kinder (Headteacher),
parents and children in the
playground.

Revd Stanley Dodd (Vicar),
Maurice Ashworth
(Headteacher). Nan Kinder
and Alan Pedley
(Governor).

New school, but old games!

Children in the new school playground fascinated by something. Wonder what it was?

Schoolchildren in Green Road just before moving to temporary quarters in Bentley Primary School while refurbishment took place. Spring 1990.

A last fling in the old playground with Deputy Headteacher Anne Burgess and Owen Hogg the caretaker.

In the 1960s an annual 'Horsefair' was held in Meanwoodside with everything from little ponies to giant Tetley drayhorses, one of which is seen here.

One of the winners with its proud owner.

In 1979 it was necessary to scaffold the church tower to carry out repairs to the spire. Peter Bewell went to see the Vicar to ask permission to climb up and take some unique shots of Meanwood. "On your own head be it", was the reply, so up he went!

Bottom of Church Lane after Brick Row was demolished, but before the Mews were built.

Greenwood Mount and the Holmwoods before Greenwood Park was built.

Allotments behind the Working Men's Club where 'The Wickets' were later built.

Looking down on the newly finished Memorial Drive roofs.

Top of Church Avenue.

A view not seen by many. A close up of the top of the spire.

The Parksides.

The famous clock. Built by E.J.Dent of London in 1850 to a design by Edmund Beckett Denison. Have you noticed that there is a clockface on only three sides of the tower? (A reference to the Trinity ?)

Birds eye view.

Albert Smith, pictured here in his robes, was a pupil at Green Road school 1908/1918. He became Lord Mayor of the City in 1972/3 and was later made an Hon. Alderman.

Albert visiting the school during his year in office.

ALAN PEDLEY D.F.C. a Meanwood man through and through. He entered politics in 1951 when he represented the Meanwood ward on the City Council and then became a West Yorkshire County Councillor. Elected Lord Mayor in 1975/6 we see him here wearing his chain of office. He was awarded the Distinguished Flying Cross for his service to the country 1939/1945 when he was Captain of a Sunderland flying boat. His numerous campaign medals are displayed in the cabinet at the top of the staircase in Leeds Civic Hall. He was involved in many community activities including many years as a governor of Green Road School. He was also Hon. President of the Meanwood Village Association until his death in 1999. He lived life to the full and one of his favourite sayings was "Life is for living".

The scene at the top of Greenwood Mount in the 1980s when construction was starting on Greenwood Park on land in front of the Beckett Nursery.

A new house under construction near the bottom of Church Lane in August 1993.

The newly built extension at the back of the Myrtle Pub in 1974.

Refurbishment of the old cottages on Parkside Road opposite the cricket ground in 1979.

Hollin Farm (formerly the Whalley Tannery, Noble's Farm, Holmes's Farm) was saved from demolition in 1977 and converted into a private dwelling.

A view of the dwelling after restoration in 1978.

1984 saw the building of the new G.T.Smith supermarket on the old Capitol site.

The Holmwood estate which was built on farmland between Church Lane and Parkside Road in the 1960s.

Steelwork being erected for the new Aldi store at the junction of Stainbeck Avenue and Stonegate Road.

Meanwood Terminus in 1967.

The original Vicarage in 1964.

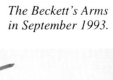

The Beckett's Arms in September 1993.

Tongue Lane Farm in 1967.

Oddy's Fold in 1967.

A side view of Meanwood Hall in 1993.

The Hall again, this time showing the frontage and gardens in the spring of 1996.

One of the hospital Villas in 1993.

A photograph depicting some of the elaborate stone carvings on the Hall.

The Lord Mayor of Leeds, Councillor Peggy White, speaking at the hospital's final gala day in June 1995.

The 'death' of the hospital in October 1997 when all the villas were demolished and the site redeveloped as a large housing estate.

The sundial on the face of Carr Manor.

The front elevation of Carr Manor in 1996.

One of the architectural gems of the Manor, an elaborately decorated plaster ceiling.

The beautiful pergola in the grounds.

Looking up to the delicate tracery of the ironwork on the pergola roof.

The view at the rear of the Methodist Church prior to the building of the Cedar Room and new toilets in 1973.

MEANWOOD METHODIST CHURCH

SERVICE OF THANKSGIVING
AND DEDICATION
on the occasion of

THE OPENING OF
THE NEW CHURCH HALL

to be known as

THE CEDAR ROOM

Saturday 10th March 1973 at 3p.m

THE OPENING BY SIR GEORGE W. MARTIN, KBE. LLD. J.P.
THE SERMON BY REV. WALKER–LEE, M.A.
Chairman of the District.
THE SERVICE CONDUCTED BY REV. E.W.R. LLOYD,
Superintendent Minister
and
REV. ERIC J. HUDSON,
Minister of the Church

The programme for the dedication of the Cedar Room.

The Sunday School Queen, Lucille Juggins, from the Methodist Church, on her way to the Gala at Crabtree's sports ground in 1960.

Julie Whitley who was the Queen in 1966 presenting a fancy dress prize to 'The Holly and The Ivy' (David and Richard Bewell).

The Methodist Church celebrated the
250th Anniversary of John Wesley with a
parade from the Church down Green
Road to Meanwoodside in 1988.

'John Wesley' arriving on horseback.
(Mary Kettlewell).

Above and on the left we see young people leaving the Methodist Church in 1981 after a service celebrating the 100th Anniversary of the Sunday School in the present building.

All dressed up for the occasion and complete with their dolls.

*Members of the
Methodist Church
congregation leaving
the service in 1981
commemorating 100
years of Methodism on
this site. (The first
chapel was at the
bottom of Church
Lane).*

Members having a chat in the schoolroom after the service, including John Sully (local preacher), Bessie Williamson, Kathryn Barratt, Pauline Daniel, Rene and Alf Greenwood, and Brian Hollingworth.

More members of the Methodist Church chatting after the Service commemorating 100 years on the present site.

Cynthia Sully with her daughters Anthea and Heather.

Joyce and Frank Whitley.

*Della Pearson,
Blanche Wallis and
Christine Bewell.*

*Geoff. and Enid
Wadsworth.*

*Richard Waterton,
Lawrence Pearson,
(rear view!), and the
Revd Stanley Rose.*

In 1993 the Methodist Church entered a float in the Lord Mayor's parade, and are pictured here on Woodhouse Moor preparing for ' the off'. The ladies at the front, Christine Bewell, Pat Eckersley and Eileen Barratt. The Church was awarded the cup for the most original entry.

All dressed up and raring to go!

Arthur Hopwood, 'The Preacher', holding forth from the pulpit with the organ in the background.

Val Lolley enjoying a laugh with the Revd Roy Newell on 14th November 1998 when he paid a return visit to open the Christmas Market. He was the Methodist Minister from 1982 until 1991.

Great excitement at the Methodist Church on June 11th 1994 when the Methodist Minister, The Revd Christopher Humble (1991-1996) married a member of the congregation, Kathryn Barratt. (now proud parents of Abigail and twins Joseph and Naomi).

The Tannery (strictly speaking in recent years it was a fellmongery, where wool is removed from hides). Photographed here just after it ceased work in June 1994. An important Meanwood employer since it was built in 1857. The chimney was a major landmark.

The frontage, with the datestone over the doorway which reads 'S 1857 S'. The S S refers to Samuel Smith who built the Tannery. His son was Samuel Smith the Tadcaster brewer.

In 1998 the developers moved in and the site is seen here in the early stages of partial demolition.

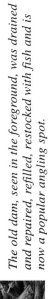

The demolition almost complete and refurbishment about to start. Most of the old stone buildings were retained and converted into houses and flats. Some new dwellings were also built around the site.

The old dam, seen in the foreground, was drained and repaired, refilled, restocked with fish and is now a popular angling spot.

In the demolition stage at the Tannery this old iron turbine was pulled out and put on a lorry ready to be sent to the scrapyard when it was spotted by a passer-by. After some desperate telephone calls to the developers it was retrieved and is now a permanent feature in the courtyard as a reminder of our industrial heritage.

One of the smaller buildings which was converted into dwellings.

The Grange, a house adjacent to the Tannery, seen here in June 1994. Originally it was Wood Mills Farm and at one time the residence of Samuel Smith who built the Tannery. Samuel is buried in Meanwood Churchyard.

In the 1999 redevelopment of the Tannery site some bungalows were built in the garden and The Grange was refurbished and fenced off.

A new approach road was built to serve the Tannery development and on the south side, on the site of a smallholding, a medical centre was constructed and named 'Millside'.

'Fairfax' the old house on Parkside Road just before the steep hill.

Valley Farm in autumn splendour in 1981. It stands at the bottom of Dunny Hill and used to face the original line of the Ring Road.

Further up Dunny Hill we see the row of cottages called The Grove, pictured in 1998.

The beck in Autumn.

The War Memorial at the bottom of the church drive where a service is still held every November.

113

Faces in the park.
Vic Bowling, Tom Marwood,
Ronald Taylor and
Jim Kent.

Peter Langley with Harry
Roberts, the ex landlord of
the Bay Horse Inn, taken
about 1970.

Some happy ladies. Jean Barker, Anne Chamley, Margaret Leiper, Doreen Wood and Lily Slade.

Ladies all in their finery at the Lord Mayor's parade in 1993.
Pat Eckersley, Christine Bewell, Cathy Barratt and Brenda Bramham.

More Meanwood ladies.
Val Milner, Barbara Blakeney, Wendy Pinder, Jackie Brewer and Janet Wenham.

Three schoolgirls on the opening day of the new Green Road School in 1993.

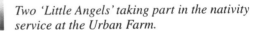

Two 'Little Angels' taking part in the nativity service at the Urban Farm.

Looking down Green Road towards the park after heavy snow in 1991.

The goit at the bottom of the Hollies in the winter of 1979.

A view from near the bottom of Dunny Hill looking towards Weetwood in the winter of 1973.

Winter sunshine and shadows in the garden of Ivy Cottage.

The parade of shops at the bottom of Stonegate Road in September 1993.

Shops at the top of Meanwood Road in September 1993.

The supermarket in Meanwood Road opposite the Health Centre in September 1993.

Oddy's Fold all boarded up prior to refurbishment.

One of the last 'White Houses'. Note the sign on the gate !

Happy schoolgirls at the Victorian Day, Green Road School in 1990.

Three of the mums doing their bit.

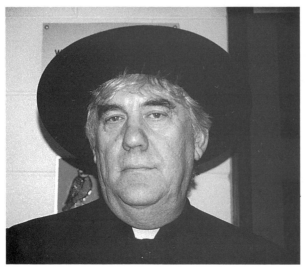

The Revd Richard Wiggen as a rather stern Victorian Vicar.

One of the teachers, Miss Lucinda Waghorn, playing her part.

Bryn Evans the Headteacher.

The Bay Horse Inn sign in Parkside Road in 1987.

The champion onion growers on the Parkside allotments in 1989. Tom Taylor, Keith Denney, Jeff. Lythe, Dennis Blenkin, Barry Radcliffe and Tom Cole. Records of the allotments go back to 20th February 1877.

The house which stands on the south side of Meanwood Cricket Club in March 1979. In earlier days only a carriageway separated the house from the deep quarry face.

All that remained of Church Farm after demolition in the 1960s. It stood in Church Lane opposite the bottom of Parkside Crescent. The site was then developed as the Holmwood estate.

ANDREW OWEN. *A Meanwood soldier who was badly burned whilst serving as a craftsman in the R.E.M.E. when his ship H.M.S. 'Sir Galahad' was bombed in the Falklands conflict in June 1982. Andrew went to Green Road School and lived in Greenwood Mount. He survived his injuries and eventually returned to his regiment, but tragically he died in an accident at work after demobilisation a few years later.*

Andrew, seen here on the left, on holiday in Scarborough with his friend Paul D'Ambrosio.

On Remembrance Sunday in London in 1983 Andrew (the tall one) laid a plaque on behalf of all the R.E.M.E. soldiers who lost their lives in the Falklands.

After his release from hospital in October 1982 Andrew returned home to Greenwood Mount for a period and is pictured here celebrating with his neighbours on his 21st birthday.

At the Meanwood Institute the committee lay on a 'Tea & Chat' event on a Sunday afternoon several times a year for elderly Meanwood residents. Transport to and from the Institute is provided where necessary and some entertainment arranged. Always popular and much appreciated by all who come along.

Seated around the table in May 1998 are.....?, Gladys Wray, Mrs. Mitton, Evelyn Danby, Kathleen Stewart and Irene Dyson.

Laura Ramsden, Bessie Williamson, Lily Betney, Edith Robinson, May Marshall, Lily Reed and Emily Dale.

Christmas carols 1998. The church choir with Christopher Rathbone the church organist.

In 1999 it was the turn of the school choir to entertain.

Tannery Square on Green Road which when threatened with demolition in 1972 prompted a protest from local people and led to the formation of The Meanwood Village Association.

Seen here in October 1974 with renovation work in hand.

The cottages were bought by The Mary Morris Housing Association, which is connected to Leeds University. The residents are mature overseas students with their families and five of the children are seen here in 1990.

Happy children playing in front of the cottages in 1990.

They were refurbished again in 1995 and a special opening took place on site with lots of music and colourful national costumes.

One of the musicians.

A happy little group playing cards in the school playground, 19th July 1991.

Happy 'prisoners' behind the new school railing in 1994. Still called Green Road by older residents, but the official title is 'Meanwood Church of England (Aided) Primary School.

A group of children from Green Road on an outing to Roundhay Park.

Hoping to play for Yorkshire!. Paul D'Ambrosio, David Bewell, Jeremy Prentice and Richard Bewell practicing in the old school playground about 1968.

Very important ladies! The headteacher with the dinner ladies in 1983.

Back row: *Olive Hampton, Brenda Horsfall, Marjorie Hopwood, Pamela Morris, Rita Durrant. Front row*: *Esme Poulter, Nan Kinder (Headteacher), Anne Corners.*

The school staff in 1989. Dianne Jones (School Secretary), John Crimp, Janine Chambers, Margaret Waud, Anne Burgess (Deputy Headteacher), Heather Booth, Bryn Evans (Headteacher), Jean David, Pat Shah Khan, Christine Croft and Margaret Taylor.

Meanwood C.of E. Primary School football team of 1988.
Front row; Bryn David, Christopher Nelson, Tony Hudson, Wayne Moore, Martin Denton
Middle row; Lee McHugh, Nicol Rorrison, Jonathon White, Lee Dobson, James Benson
Back row; Gareth Sessions, Carl Walsh, Marc Fisher, Bilal Al-Khaffaf, Luke Phelan.

Meanwood C.of E. Primary School netball team of 1987.
Front row; Clare Smith, Gail Jackson, Lynn Hartshorne, Hannah Wilson, Claire Ketlewell.
Back row; Nichola Queenan, Joanne Sollitt, Anna Benson.

Meanwood in recent years has been the setting for numerous television programmes such as 'The Darling Buds of May', 'A Touch of Frost', etc. Pictured here is a film crew outside Tannery Square filming an episode of 'Barbara'.

Not just the professionals! M.V.A. Deputy Chairman Doreen Wood is a keen movie-maker and has recorded many events in the area over a number of years. Probably her most well known is a highly entertaining film depicting the antics of some local squirrels. She is pictured here with her husband Frank coming out of the Methodist Church with her equipment in 1984.

top left: The Destructor chimney being demolished brick by brick in August 1977.

top right: The Tannery chimney being scaffolded prior to demolition in 1998.

left: CRASH! Down comes the chimney at Bateson's Tannery on a foggy dark day in the sixties or seventies...? This is where the Netto supermarket now stands.

HEPWORTH CUP   1993

(scorer)   (Sugar)
Row: A. Walton, A. Daniels, S. Leonard, D. Turner, C. Carden, S. Jackson, S. Crossland
Row: M. Bray, S. Bray, K. Jones(capt), S. Dobson, A. Bowes, J. Walwin.

Members of Woodhouse Cricket Club celebrating the winning of the Hepworth Cup.

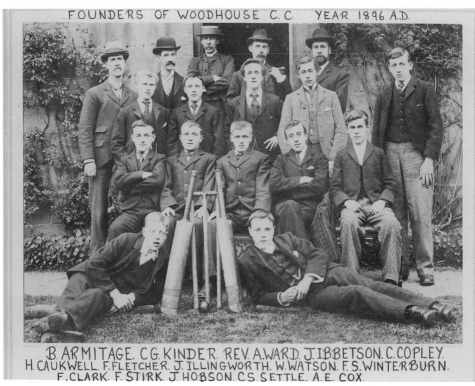

FOUNDERS OF WOODHOUSE C.C.   YEAR 1896 A.D.

B. ARMITAGE. C.G. KINDER. REV. A.WARD. J. IBBETSON. C. COPLEY.
H. CAUKWELL. F. FLETCHER. J. ILLINGWORTH. W. WATSON. F. S. WINTERBURN.
F. CLARK. F. STIRK. J. HOBSON. C.S. SETTLE. A.E. COX.

This is really a photograph that belongs in Volume 1, but it has just come to light and is too good to miss. Woodhouse Cricket Club again, but way back in 1896 when the Club was founded.

Highbury Cricket Club. Division 2A champions in 1986.
Back row; S.Harvey (scorer), J.Horton, R.Harvey, S Rosenthall, R.Briggs, C.Briggs, I.Langstaff.
Front row; S.Dobson, D. Harvey, J.Moyles (Captain), R.Langstaff, I.Rowlands (Vice Captain).
Plus mascot!

Meanwood Cricket Club Juniors .
Back row; Niall Barker, Robert Child,
Chris Warner, Drew Blyth-Dobson.
Middle row; Adam Deedigan, Will Edson,
Jack Nichol, Liam Morris, Mathew Morris.
Front Row; Kieron Barker, Jordan Morris.

Meanwood Cricket Club team in the early/mid
seventies.
Back Row; Peter Langley, Phil Dyson,
Steve Shires, Jeff. Shires, Roger Anderson,
Rob Guthrie, Andy Duckett.
Front Row; Vic Banner, Chris Roe,
Mick Dews, Colin Murgatroyd, Mal Denney.

142

Brenda Lancaster, who lived in Meanwood for many years, being congratulated by Paddy Ashdown on her election to Leeds City Council in 1999. She became the Deputy Lord Mayor of Leeds in 2004/5.

Harold Best (in blue shirt) was elected as the Member of Parliament for Leeds N.W. in 1997. He was born and brought up in Meanwood, went to Bentley Lane School and was a wolf cub at the Methodist Church. Prior to being an M.P. he served on the West Yorkshire County Council from 1981 until 1986. Our picture shows him at the opening of the Millside Medical Centre in 1998.

CHEERS! In February 1993 Martin Cockerill was pestered by his two daughters to start a ladies football team, so he formed the 'Meanwood Vixens' and became their manager. Ruth captained the team and is pictured here having a welcome drink at half time. They were very successful and rapidly expanded, with  *teams ranging from 7 year olds to open age. They changed the name to 'Leeds City Vixens' and became National Champions in 1994 & 1995 and World Champions in 1999 & 2000. Ruth also became an England netball player.*

Every year a Harvest Festival is held in Meanwood Methodist Church and our picture here shows the flowers and fruit on display in the 1960s.

A lovely colourful picture to finish off with. Peggy Ashton in Meanwood Parish Church with her display in the Flower Festival marking the 150th anniversary celebrations in 1999.